MW01480647

Be happy for this moment. This
moment is your life.

— Omar Kayyam

This above all: to thine ownself be true.

– Shakespeare

Excellence is not an act, but a habit.

– Aristotle

No act of kindness, no matter how small, is
ever wasted.

– Aesop

The way to be happy is to make others so.

- Robert Ingersoll

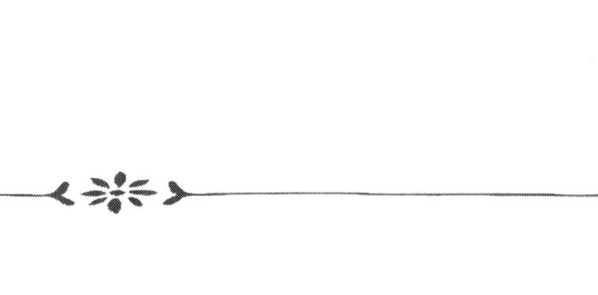

Each of us is limitless; each of us with his
or her right upon the earth.

– Walt Whitman

Peace is always beautiful.

– Walt Whitman

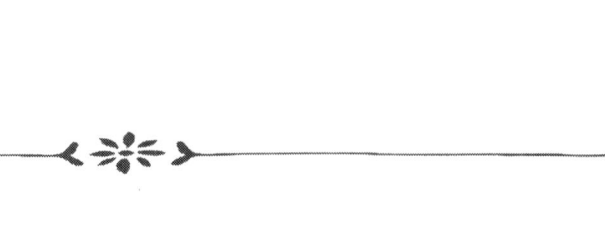

The greatest mistake you can make in life
is to be continually fearing you will make
one.

— Elbert Hubbard

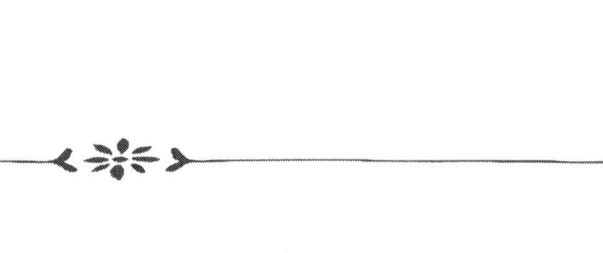

Bloom where you are planted.

- 1 Corinthians KJV

Made in the USA
Middletown, DE
13 June 2018